PANCAKES FOR NEPTUNE

PANCAKES FOR NEPTUNE

OWEN BULLOCK

RECENT
WORK
PRESS

Pancakes for Neptune
Recent Work Press
Canberra, Australia

Copyright © Owen Bullock, 2023

ISBN: 9780645651249 (paperback)

A catalogue record for this
book is available from the
National Library of Australia

Cover image: Sarah Julie via unsplash, Dominic Wade Photography
reproduced under Creative Commons licence 2.0
Cover design: Recent Work Press
Set by Recent Work Press

recentworkpress.com

PH

For Geoffrey Lee Cooper

Contents

Pancakes for Neptune

I'm making pancakes for Neptune—
his funding was cut in the last round
and I wanted to show support
for his long-term commitment
to the maritime community

142 scholarships in the last twelve years alone—
some deprived souls
wouldn't have run away from home
and never been found
if not for his intervention

he's an acerbic character
but his smile makes me tender
he has a subtle, congenial handshake—
I'm making him some pancakes

Heat

fresh food
expensive
the water doesn't taste good

another cyclone up the coast
three varieties of apples in the supermarket
the valley too dry
to camp there

bees are dying
but they love rosemary
which flowers
most of the year

the physics of climate trend
can't be altered
some say
but what about
a quantum leap

countries must
individuals do

cycling to work
feeling better on less meat

opening up the disused car factory
to make solar panels
inviting the Mayor

A Permablitz day (10-4)

Rob taught us the bindings
for the bamboo tripods
with flax or string
Rose designed the trellis
of hazelnut switches
James dismantled pallets
and Hugo turned them into compost bins
Sue organised the double-digging
of veggie beds
Trish & team moved and planted fruit trees
twenty-eight people came together
to work, learn, share company

by the end of the day
compost bins cooking
fruit trees mulched
veggie beds full of seedlings
irrigation installed

Marie, whose garden it is
and a novice
now eats from it each day
studies organics
teaches her neighbours
about food

Diagnosis

thrush
endometriosis . . .
a female critic
told a woman writer
that the gory details of hysterectomy
should not be discussed
in a story
and I wondered . . .
since details seem vital
to an understanding

a male poet
and occasional editor
told me
women's issues
weren't universal enough

but because women represent
52% of the population in some places
I thought they might be

Brigadoon

Clarence and Marion. The steep path to the door. The view of a distant ocean and near clay tips. High tea spread to all corners of the table. Marion's bosomed embrace. Clarence's cheerful enquiry. You visit their son's pigeon loft, with its 68 varieties, some rare. He races them and sometimes wins and coos over their homecoming. And the son who stayed to nurse his mother when their father died, the last man to leave the village as houses tumbled into the pit. The Kendalls', the Stephens', the Bullocks', the Shorts', the Browns', all scooped out, from *Avalon* to *Brigadoon*, *Kenwyn* the last resistance, until that son chose a new house a few miles north and named it . . .

Animate and full of spirits

As the night, as the Chapel when you thought it housed a ghost. As the hedge where he lurked to scare you. Where the other brother stepped on a snake. For ever after, these are the scare places. You called out "Nee-al!!!" in two long syllables at the pub and he jumped as if his father summoned him from some long dead country, the boy who had not tended the well.

Precipice

Alone at the edge. What alone, what precipice. The ground beneath a slab, stair jutting out, space to breathe, fears to form, two hundred, three hundred feet, is it—fifteen enough to kill. The family back away, wander off. Confront silence. With their mother and visitors, safe, young legs sure (except that one moment on the pancakes). A falcon hovers into place above the bluff, shifts to reconnoitre, returns with ecstatic ease to the same vantage. Confront altitude. Try to think of this as a moment. A granite slab wedged beneath. Could fall. Any time. It sat for millennia. I'm 35. What could? Will fears to leave but like any possessed they return to the headland with heath and hawthorn stumped.

A place for the Phantom

The Phantom got away (again). A train to Liverpool, he bribed passage to Australia. A tiny porthole, seasickness twisting his body into half a man, and half again—many's the time he thought he was dying. The ship in early, he disembarked on a rope. Spent six months scrimping, delivering pizza. Gave himself up to the authorities and was pardoned. Went back to music: church organ, retro bands, teaching, and after five years a steady gig. Hear him each Sunday at the Carillon on Lake Burley-Griffin with those other-worldly bells.

Ancient and modern

for Paul Collis

The ancestor's language falls like rain, settles. Heat escapes the air.

You, the child, ground the elder—a surprise that hops away like mimicry.

You take the lift and as doors open into the red land, the red land comes flooding into you—only your grandfather's fine rain keeps you from choking. You open your eyes in defiance of the sting. City blocks assemble. You find your way to the fireside, the two-bar heater, the space buzzing with dry or sickly discourse.

Options

Clothes laid out on a table in the opshop. I pick up a huge pink jersey, hear a lady say, 'I knitted that'. Giggles as I try it on, and another the same colour that's far too small. I hook a gauzy grey dress over myself—'I made that, too'. Shuffle around to a mirror in the middle of the shop. The dress has changed: it's blue with cartoon panels, including an image of Mickey Mouse. Short, slightly puffed sleeves. Sleek, makes my stomach look flat. I hop up and down in front of the mirror. Shoppers edge away, overly absorbed in cast-offs, but with staring children. I don't want to leave the mirror. I don't want to take the dress off. The shop is suddenly cluttered with chairs. I can't return the dress to the table. I carry on gazing. What kind of shoes?

> little boy
> on the plane, looking for
> the magic

Judging comps

Fashion

He's wearing robes, cerise, magenta, loosely draped like wind
on the shore—you can garden in them, even fix the downpipes.
Kilts energised and free, leaf vein yellow, flame and midnight
blue. Lavalavas, passionfruit and the light in an orchard at midday.
Men will dress this way from now on. I give the designers eleven
out of ten.

Cookery

You can't go wrong with Indian spices, so long as you know
how to prepare them and they're fresh and they do. Garam masala
and lots of it, not much chilli, just enough to feel the bite. They
give me sensation. I reward them with a trip to Paris to see two
of the pinnacles of western culture: a Frenchwoman smoking a
cigarette and a Frenchman mounting a bicycle. If they win the
final round, they'll go back in time to gold platforms, glitter and
Gibson guitars—the era so holy we do not name it.

NY

I arrive at the party and get talking with a woman standing in a circle of men. She's playing a card game with them, I tell her her hand is great. I push forward a bag on the floor that's in my way, not realising it's a signal in the game. 'You just lost me a lot of money,' she says. About $70. 'The least you can do is buy us all a drink.' The round comes to $120. I send the drinks over from the bar without rejoining them. I'm just leaving when the host hands me a $100 bill. 'That was too much,' he says. 'You're not going?' 'Just looking for someone.' I think about stealing a coat from the cloakroom, like the character in *Can you ever forgive me?* but can't bring myself to do it. Outside I call a cab. I don't want to repeat the convoluted journey across the city by subway—with my luck tonight I'd get mugged. I give the cabbie the name of the hotel. 'That's a long way, pal, cost you $70.' 'Fine.' I decide to give him the hundred dollar bill and tell him to keep the change. Someone texts me, asking why I'm not at the party. 'Unwell, going home.' The cabbie harps on about nothing much. I change my mind about the tip. Opposite the hotel, a bookshop opens late. I head inside and ask for a book by Ron Padgett, hoping to find the poems from the movie *Paterson*, go back to the hotel and start reading.

Not knowing

these lines on the road . . .
I want to stop
and work out what they mean
but the flow of traffic says
drive

shapes on my shirt
don't tell me what they are
only blues and yellows
yellows and browns
I wore them for years—
before someone pointed out
cars
          and pineapples

Caroline Myss says
native Americans
had nothing to compare Columbus' ship to
so they didn't see it

but I don't know
about the past
history
a fabled agreed upon

or the lines on the road
shapes on my shirt

Welcome to the tables

down to the bone
the fish woman's gills
massaged open

marauded
the body
blade-ankled

concerning
the back smooth
or feet disjointed

hollow eyes
its end
beginning

a clay mind
by trepanning fingers
released

Erode

for Cori

she folds her body forward
eyes fall into rivers
her head rests on the mountain
hair streams down its sides
teeth clatter through valleys
legs split into fissures
toes roll in a rill
she lets out three final breaths
and a crack spreads across the synclines
   of her face

O

my father said a child
should be a man
when he could
make a woman make a man

my mother said a child
should stay a child
for as long as
she could hold him by her hand

Chasing the moon

for Sue

followed you
till I exhausted myself
you walked, ran
flew five years
I had to be alone
but you were there
in a dream
the children we looked after
bouncing on the bed—
I've told it before
the dream's become a story

it shines no light

will you return
next quarter
will I make it
to where you are?
what will it cost me?
I am . . .
I am

the meditation you announced
the silence we share
covers me

Swipe

I point at myself
with more vigour
and consistency
than I condemn
or notice
you

*

what will be a hand
emerges from dark waters
to step
on two stones
causeway
to an island

*

art gallery
your reflections
my pebble

*

through the valley of death
before summer
strikes

*

city lights
the heron
bewildered

*

a child on the way
the line fractured
the line maintained

*

walking uphill
walking uphill

down falling sky

*

remember me

do not remember me

for long

The flower you left for me

pink veins
        temple and breast
stamens
        and smiles burst
from petals

hair arms to torso
how they serve
    the body
    bloom

Four chairs

the general sat in white wicker
planning the attack
smiling at you over tea
talking about the tractor's engine
a strange bird cry heard in the night

the director relaxed and pushed back
the crucial shot captured
he wanted to surf the place he occupied
with uncertainty as a board

the nursing teacher eased a right turn
as she asked the young apprentice
why did you want to be a nurse?

the boy sat for his birthday treat
waited
till the alarm rang
on his childhood
in an empty tin

Shoebox

notebooks
that refused to become anything

birth certificates
letters of thanks
unusable adaptors
a picture of Mozart by a five-year-old
a white feather
a rare letter from father
calligraphied lines from Blake
the key for tuning the drum

a guarantee

Returning, I check that things remain

van Gogh's chair
in the National Gallery

earts in the lanes

white peaks as you approach
St Austell

stone hot water bottles
for sale
in the Market House

    this time
    the Market House
    closed

The Greensplat road

beyond the laced shoes of town houses
shops boarded up
past drains and streams   below the viaduct

Trenance Hill   1 in 3
mossy walls   dense hawthorns
the bend   that twists cars

get your breath   on the flat
in a swell   of dappled light
eerie songs   in holes under hedges

higher   to open fields
milk crates   signs for cabbages
climb the swerve and cluster of hedges
scramble for earts   tease a handful

at iron gates   span the eyes
each blade and trace   the ground under your feet
you feel like you own it

up where a burra
was first to face the town
a trail where houses sulked
on the way home   roaming   lost   at 2 a.m.

looking back   the sea seven miles hence
the tiny hamlet's dwellings   set like leaves
either side the stem

the blockworks   the turning to the new road
that's been there twenty years
Greensplat Pit   its conical mound
conveyor belts   digger rumble
the chapel and phone box   where kids made crank calls

past Wheal Martyn
the track you can no longer circumnavigate
hoses burning   after the one o'clock blast
passing places   houses
your own a ruin
father dead   mother moved on
the apricots he planted
nestle in a thicket   below the burra
that towered over us

willows   brambles   furze
you snag on everything
stumble   in the rubble

three-quarters of a mile away
above disused Gunneath Pit
the sign still reads   *Greensplat ¾*

The way we do things round here

fifteen years or more
coughing your lungs out
until, four days in hospital
they finally emptied

tough, my brother said
one of the hard men, lean
half a stone heavier than you ran
at naval school

you never complained
except about the government
and that didn't count   to me
Arthur Scargill some kind of hero
to you   Thatcher the ultimate villain
along with the Queen and Prince—
we never had spells or wands
just tinsel at Christmas
best enjoyed alone

when you eyed that twinkle
I liked you, but only drink
or the thought of a pretty woman
seemed to conjure it, and she was
never mother   never, father—
what had she done?

I sought you out
you wrote to me

about the treatment
and as you shrank
stopped walking to the pub
each evening, took the car, that
ill-begotten thing on wheels
or accepted a lift
and choked on it till breakfast

the birds came and your
cat's fond bell
herbs and onions

you survived
in the house without hot water
toilet at the bottom of the garden
where it belongs
and now now, I second
your fine ideals, father

Dear Mother,

I worked out why I love cream: you craved it when you were pregnant. I'm grateful for the jumpers you knitted me, though they didn't always fit. I relished the way you played with words, without knowing you were. You had your own grammar; I based my Cornish story on the way you spoke. I'm glad you cherished daffodils, I could gather some from the bank. You asked me to pick earts for the pie—more time in the hedges. It intrigued me that you had friends—I didn't know how. You told people on the phone I was clever. You had a phone voice, putting back in all the aitches you normally dropped, and some hextra ones. I'm sorry I fought with you when I was 14. You could always get the better of me by pulling my hair. You told me I was never meant to be born, you wanted another girl, you were tired, sitting with your head back, a flannel across your brow, eating blood oranges. Thanks for the Leeds United kit, sewing band patches on my denim jacket, for the money to go to football and gigs, for playing with my kids, making them mice from folded hankies like you used to do for me, having the password 'cup of tea' to come into your caravan when you stayed, for the knitted bumbletubs you sent when they were little, odds n ends from the opshop. Thanks for asking me to take you on a trip to Mevagissey in your chair, the last outing we had together in a blue-watered, double-harboured heaven.

From your son,
Owen

From here to there and almost back

waiting to go
your eyelashes more mascara
at the ends

airport lounge
a young man chews a sandwich
magnanimously bored

tax & duty free
your face
a place to rest

watching you flick
through a fashion magazine
my judgements all wrong

summer rains—
the door of the graveyard
stands open

how I want my gravestone to look
overgrown
like this rose bush

a solitary pigeon
where the waterwheel
once turned

Grasmere
reflections soft as rain
on water

tea on the lawn
an old man watches
a miniscule bird

holidays—
we complain about
what we normally do

a duck's wake
takes me
in

dawn
my dead brother's spirit
and a melody

summer garden
a poppy petal
tumbles

halfway
up the ornamental wall
a snail

cliffwalk
I cool my forehead
with dew from a leaf

granite fireplace
the age
in me

your restless sleep . . .
keeping
still

their wall
in Truthwall
bright yellow

airport—
as we walk, you straighten
my collar

UK

Dunfermline's like a mini Edinburgh
multicultural caffees and stuff, ken

have you come far?
to befriend the arsonist

I'll wear a bikini
to listen to Vivaldi's Summer

p cannot validate q

it's like the beginning of a hologram

painted or unpainted
buckled, unbuckled

I would have changed the loudness of London

serviettes on the floor

grey quartz and black tourmarine
ivy and valerian

a seat named after them

ants might get me fingers!

beer is food

no animals to attract
or defend themselves from

we're outdumbered

another sock in the road

are you a collector or a classifier?

swell & surge
slip & skip

every man and his dog's got a dog

the chattering classes

I don't know what ta-boo-lay *is*

Swiftly see each moment flies
See and learn be timely wise
Every moment shortens days
Every pulse beats time away
This the every heaving breath
Wafts onto eternal death   (Anon)

kneeding & clawing

nettles & stones

he also believed in other more dodgy things like
honesty and goodness

Crabber's Nip

they have the correct apple pie to custard ratio
the best fish 'n' chips so far

power lines
moss dangles

  treasure every sighting

    I never stopped wanting to be sophisticated

     in the supermarket twilight zone
     me and Brian Clough were crocodile ghostbusters

to celebrate the nooks & crannies
of god

  a laster

    you can buy sexy mother-pucker lipstick

    Buddha irradiates the wonderful energies of Healing,
    Luck, Abundance and Happiness eternally.

jewels in church and temple
ourselves manifested

No! Smoking

   Mixxed Vegetables

sultry noise

Dwellings

cathedral
please enter
via another door

courtyard
feet echo
feet

doors closed
a squirrel
on duty

the priest
skips up the flagged steps
two at a time

catechism
I believe . . .
in as little as possible

looking up
at the vast ceiling—hammocks
for refugees?

lilies
a dangerous
scent

*

cool breeze
robes on the Buddha's statue
ruffle

a pair of socks
draped
on the bonsai

beware
pick-
pockets

the orange-robed monk
teaches
through a loud-hailer

Tongue

Masonic lodges aren't noted for their indoor outdoor flow

a lot of linen suits in the Canberra poetry scene

my dreams aren't good enough
I dreamed I was boiling pasta

I don't know why I'm exerting pressure

as soon as you get a boyfriend
you stress

can mung beans go so wrong?

my kids are trying to kill me

he even argued under water

life's too short for a dollar coin in the trolley

the missing chunks of god

not all my zombies are carnivores

I still want to go to the footy and have fun

my boyfriend
not my boyfriend . . .

I get it

you're invited by the way
there's gonna be like a dance

a drop dead date

Training

a line and a smudge

Craig's a very jealous person

there's training for desk politics

did Andy Warhol have a comb-over?

angels play table tennis . . .

kunst kunst

no one forgoes the lyric

Vegan lip balm

Dear Burglar
We Forgive You

Sitting

after Ryōkan

a yellowhammer lands on a rock
water gleaming

I can't follow the path of ripples
on the stream

among brown cows
one black cow

sparrows and mynahs pick at the ground
where cows have been

how slowly
can I walk through the meadow

koromiko we planted
next to koromiko that came up

scratch marks on the old totara
where the possum scurries

clothes in bundles
in the gypsy wagon

plans to read
but the river more inviting

what passes
glimpsing what passes

A 1 not a 2

sick with flu
I email my supervisor
to say I won't be in tomorrow
and text her to be sure
she got the message

return phone call
crackly line
me woolly-headed
she says I'm nice to her face
but disrespect her
I should make more of an effort
the class tomorrow is important
I can come late and leave early

she rings back, tells me not to come in
she has papers for the students
demands I apologise next time I see her
tells me I'm a fucking idiot

rings again
will you play table tennis with me
tomorrow?
I can't because I'm sick
I'll kick your fucking head in, mate
I tell her not to ring again

wrong number

like a lot of people
stamping their feet

Toyscape

a ball, yellow, blue
       soft when you touch it
hard when it hurtles through the air
         when you want to roll it on your skin
to take your pulse, temperature

splits apart, gathers around you
       like a pair of ear muffs
plays Bach on wind chimes
       multiplies so you can juggle
          split the space/time continuum
so you have more time

rockets at high speeds like an axe
       splits wood for the elderly
orbits the sun to trick astronomers
        lands in the sea and bounces on the surface
         to summon fish
make tsunamis for whaling ships

lands on the moon, bounces back
       to show NASA
        what a waste of time it is exploring space
circles Saturn, bounces back
       to show NASA what a waste
        of time it is
         exploring outer space

jumps into the chests of rocket scientists
to help them go within

The package

wrapped in multi-coloured paper
in the shape of a citadel

unwrapped
shrinks to a small pyramid

receivers fiddle with the object
for a few moments
finding a door which slides open
to reveal a pebble, rust red

held in the hand, contemplated
it warms and cools
explodes into particles of jet-blue dirt
that descend like slow glitter
onto faces and hands
settling in like skin cream
no change perceived

over the next few days
they laugh at inappropriate times
sing to strangers on the street
tame the tidal waves of looks
with glad eyes

people they meet
disclose things about themselves they never told anyone
cancer cells atrophy
blockages in arteries clear

singing softly
in the privacy of mirrors
stories of love
and days of loss
that brought them to their finest moments

they raise a chorus of children
singing *Biko*
by Peter Gabriel
into all the hatreds of the world

Dressing

sick of your wardrobe
use the floordrobe

do you know how tricky it is to handle an M16 with fake fingernails?

at ice hockey you're that far away from men hitting each other with sticks

we made paper darts of the church newsletter

I'm going to eat my bizarre vegan sandwich

sewing to death-metal

me mincers are packin' up
[mince pies: eyes]

he unfollowed me

I don't want to control alt delete today

dirt on the windows
light makes cobwebs filigree

I want my mama!

some of my best friends are words

the shallow basket brimming with vegetables

this room stinks ~~bad~~ of ~~sandlealwood and mediocrity~~ sailors

we never know when someone's listening

my husband calls me mum

not special *in a negative way*

it's never too late to get bendy

is that a bag?!

happy is buying

I'm going to die tonight, see

maybe after, I'll be very employable

Reel

we have to prioritise our tantrums

　　on my to do list: choose happiness

　　　　fifty years later she realised
　　　　she'd been beautiful
　　　　in the place where you ate
　　　　ice cream with forks

　　　　we turn into reflections

　　　　　it's not tea-towel over your shoulder time any more

　　　　　I have no heart, just a stupid brain

　　　　　did ee put sugar?

　　　　　when you buy it you want it

　　　　　　I'll be back now chef!

　　　　　　　he's a bit on the spectrum or something

　　　　　　hey, why don't you sit down and play us that
　　　　　　Fire Hose Reel

　　　　　I won't eat your bagel

　　　　the pigeon wants to mate with me

　　　　the scent of daffodils along the corridor . . .

　　　looking down is another way of looking behind

　　high heels in the sand

a man wandered out into the day and said
possibly

　　I'll be five minutes early for destiny

The last

hearing Keijiro Suga

feet of cement sprout out of the jungle
pools of concrete expand, merge
pillars cover trees, warehouses, palaces
roads plaster the earth
sheets of roofing replace the canopy

it's perfect

the last sprig of berries coated with glass
I starve to death

Reversed

you were the first to make eye contact

let's be the suck-ups at the front

Federal Highway
she thought the sign read
Bush anger

deals with feels

she went to move her hand   and her other hand moved

that just about sums up our relationship

I can see by the hinges on your door   that you're at work

you have so many hastes still

I actually had an Oscar Wilde moment in my life

LOL must have meant lots of love

3 a.m.
you rub my back
let me get to sleep

Palliative care access
use Flemington Road
Swirl catering

their old crackers   still there

I don't want any events near me tomorrow

this flip went to Castlemaine

sweet smell
furtive schoolboys
smoking

      another four clicks   and you're there

            partial yeah!

                  the system's changing

                            I'm forced into being passive/aggressive

Unite

lovers write at the bus station

the diet's going really well

I'm rushing through my rest

you haven't got your poetry trousers on

you're not going to like what I'm saying

give up power

there'll be a lot of moon shit

why are you travelling to Tokyo?

at the end there's an orange bucket

I can't stand any kind of change

this is my last year at Uni—
what am I going to do?

beards have only got another five years,
I reckon

I like boy talk
except when they talk about sport

did you get the silence?

please don't @ me

he likes it when they break up with him
rather than he have to . . .

Psych out

I went to church for a year and it took me twenty years to get over it

the craziest people I've known have been psychologists

that reminds me I need to write to the union

when all the debts are wearing silk

she asked him out and he was like
only if you don't take drugs

no events for the next two days

drib by drab

what a stupid thing the future is
who thought of it anyway?

they would teach it each year
as if everyone forgot

our parties end with cups of tea

Sustainability quiz

cypress leaves
brush cool
against skin

in the heat
ants traverse
the mound

his sneeze through the tunnel ...
jazz trumpet

the butterfly as though
it doesn't know the way

shade of trees
bigger than
a family

summer walks ...
looking forward
to the scrunch of leaves

under trees
the scent
of burial

at the lake
the water's
nine millionth lap

snagged
on native grasses
a sustainability quiz

the butterfly
colours
a man's feet

basketball hoop
the hopeful lunge

apartments
fuck the skyline

Gingko in May

for Alison Land

no need to tread softly
through the leaves
cockatoos feeding

waves slapping
waves   slapping
the five tones

a duck's beak
smiling by

into the glare
of the dying sun
silhouettes of birds

a purple ribbon
in the bare oak—
have I forgotten you?

the light
from miles away
in your eyes

fledgling seagull—
I was young
yesterday

A line of geese

she's combing her hair
in a field of grass

a line of geese
their necks
on the horizon

a leaf
round and around
in the eddy

now that
the little boy's gone
no little wheelbarrow

she prays in the name
of the mother, the daughter
and the holy ghost

30th birthday—
his remote control plane
dances in a gale

holiday
scrabble scores muddled up
with poetry

we call it summer
a shimmer passes
through the ponga frond

one foot in . . .
a slow ripple
spreads from the bank

underwater
the shadows of green
dragonflies

in the middle of a field
raffle ticket D

since yesterday
the koru
unfolded

Feeders

in and out
with the jetsam
bread bag tie

curly feathers
on the black swan's tail—
spring solitude

mallard
wake-ing to the feeder
on the shore

pekin ducks,
black swans, greybacked gulls
wind through rocks

throwing broccoli
for ducks, a little boy says
emerald

left on a rock . . .
the children chant
crack the egg! crack the egg!

a kid
leans on a stranger
to scratch his feet

Lady of the gentle bombardment

for Christian Bök

The church of funghi frisks the rainbow
for its amino acids and 50c pieces,
breaks down the coins and sings an arrow
winged like a bomb to fuse and appease
the lady who set fire to noise and lamplight,
who asks you to join her, though you fear handcuffs,
your isolation in the ward's long night,
trussed by straps and the torch's bluff.

Her face appears on sliding strings,
follow her will across gorge and water
to redoubts hidden deep among seedlings
and the false assumptions with which you thought her.

You begin your work, rehearsing blind lanterns
till proteins meld and stained glass ripens.

Ayoub

didn't take a walk
                    home
didn't take a rest

couldn't find a kin
                    match
couldn't take a test

wouldn't let the ease
                    come
wouldn't balk the tough

shouldn't be at home
                    here
mustn't have enough

took a
            position just to fight it
hit a
            limit working solo

crossed an
            ocean to extend a
passion
            with a raking kick

did take a risk
                    and
did follow through

           can make a
                       plan happen
           can beckon you

           would let a bun
                           dance
           would be working hard

           should find the glori-
                               ous
           must future come

Skim (segmentivity, indeterminacy, components, messing with)

for Ali Jane Smith

1.
it looked like the objects would fall out of the sky
   held by two ticker hands
      a spring sprung out of case
         your single line catching

if ridicule could swamp episode 3
   posts would wire the message
      a staple, a mouse
         rephrasing plausible

dining with half a table, half a chair
   you might put socks on one leg
      fold free of all but a hinge
         .5 of a tumbler, open sandwich

2.
bread dust falls to one side of your plate
   each speck a note for art
      they sing like chairs flicked aside
         impose the new pattern

dreadlocks the coolest place
   so much you mumble around him
      but he likes you even without a radio
         will call you Polish and dance

a wild night of love becomes two decades of teasing
     out from the covers a subtle dig
          words approve the scene
               but fail the arm test for choice

3.
in the bureau of locks
     we don't like drawers full of associations
          or evidence of letters, however impressive
               we disparage stories

stories mean you own something
     know the characters
          even if you edit them out
               having proofed

you don't come at hurdles like a westerner
     roots in the bush, fallen logs
          record you good as any speaker—
               you'll answer to them

Originary

push the noise away
father and son through the desert

light comes   from many directions

one
looks at the other's ink blots
wondering if they're better

first
learn rules of engagement
(no one remembers to tell you)

they look alike   they're the same height
but they're not

they have the same haircut
but they don't

                    the castle
                                    hangs in the air
         a studded abyss

         an exterior surface   D-rings

    that won't let you in
                                    spikes   keep off

    a padded seat   but no sitting

                    the citadel
                    empty

we
killed
the gods—
what god
survives?

our names
written
on
a
plinth
in stone a dozen times

Riding

> taking them for a ride
> a helicopter
> at the showgrounds

The President focuses on 'getting bad people out of this country.' To build a wall again, a wall around Mexico.

> a magpie
> to the end of a cross pole
> launches

'Get out of my country,' the gunman says in a bar in Kansas, as he shoots and kills an Asian Indian man who'd lived and worked in America for years. A local trying to intervene is wounded. The gunman flees the interstate border. Eventually he's arrested. His eyes dead. His mouth miserable, turned down. A helicopter whirrs in the distance.

A tribute to neo-Liberalism

The library tells me they sent the journals to an offsite storage facility. They consulted faculty before they removed them from the shelves. I ask around, no one was consulted.

Another set of journals goes missing. A woman who works in the library tells me the first set was pulped—these will have gone the same way. She describes a collection of books that disappeared, how she faught for them first. 'You do realise some of these are the only copies in Australia,' she said to them. They looked at her like she was an idiot.

Clouds arch, green and black; the air turns cold. A red hand reaches out, grabs my throat. One slit from that claw and I'd be a gonner.

Driving

it helps to be feeling unhappy
when you drive the car
so you can concentrate
and not be excited by flowers
or possible worlds
which make it difficult to notice exit signs
& road markings

I try to screen out signs
too much information
but not when I'm unhappy
then I give them my obsessive attention
I accept the signs
like awkward cousins
I do what they want me to do

I like it when I'm unhappy
and find driving easier
normally, I hate driving the car

Karaoke poem

I've just walked in
  late for the party
    the host thrusts a laminated card in my hand
      asks me to sing

a man I've never met
  dressed in a kimono (all reds and pinks)
    and a curly blonde wig says
      I've been waiting for you to come and sing with me
      how about . . . 'Up where we belong'

it's a chance to try out a Joe Cocker impersonation
  I start off as Jennifer Warnes
    and we switch part way along

I didn't plan to do Karaoke
  it's like
walking into a pet shop and coming out
  with a monkey

you channeled Joe Cocker
  it was a gift to the world

I never got to see him
  but now I have

I heard him in Sydney
  you were just like him

I drink two glasses of water
walk over the bridge
catch the bus home

who knows what tomorrow brings

Music is poetry

When Dave Gilmour flies into the green light, his pinch harmonics the shrieks of selves on Comfortably Numb. When Patti Smith screams freedom to My Generation. When Doug Pettibone grooves through Lucinda Williams' Out of Touch with his yellow firebird, soloing songs within song—she gives him a hug and a kiss when the poem completes itself, and he shucks a little smile.

Ashes

your Ashes to Ashes
clown costume said
this one human
can be many

but we learnt the catechism:
go to Uni, get a job

> *oh you look strange in that*

> *men don't usually wear colour*

> *you're all the same you alternative types*
> *play music, act and juggle*

> *have you made up your mind yet*
> *whether you're a poet or a musician?*

instructions kept coming:

> *can you tone it down a bit?*

> *could you please not write so much?*

> *you can't try on her fur coat*

till we accepted too many compromises
(innovation like a sweaty costume)

but some days
when we slice a few minutes off the clock
open another tab, flash up a track:

'Putting out Fire with Gasoline'

'Life on Mars'

'Fly'

tears come streaming back
(the tears someone stole)
with the absolute knowledge
this one human
can be many

Letter to Oscar

Prelude—the book speaks

I was tree, pulped in the paper mill in Hertford
a memory like a family taken away

I was shaped, layered, bound, lined
and others like me used for numbers

for the stock, the takings, sales
but I was lucky and given to this young man

they called Oscar—I never knew his real name
he told me stories in pictures

his mob, the sails that came, beaches
the station and the town swells, the native

police boys doing their duty hanging their kin
it poured onto me with tears

that have faded and all that's left is me
holding the sticks of his scattered life

this is all I know

*

Dear Oscar,
           Granfer came across your book
when he went to Australia for the mine
and met Mr Anscombe, friend of Dr Boge
who showed it to him, he copied some pictures
he likes to draw, he makes they books
where you flick the page and a little man
dances or a snake climbs up a ladder
we got adders here, I see you got snakes
and apparently they'm killers
Granfer's a engineer and went to install a pump
like Trevithick's in a place called Ballarat
and in Melbourne he saw where
7 Cornishmen on the *Mystery* landed, 1855

     *

#1 Sub Inspector and Troopers shooting

is this the police? they all got guns
and one of em saddled on a horse with a bushy tail
they'm fierce, some with horrible moustaches
and all the little birds by the pond
one of the men takes aim, not for a bird
but your father maybe, what's to do?
did he run? did they chase un?
did he steal a horse, is that why you'm there
watching?
        they got spurs on their boots
like the Wild West and bindings by their knees
just like old man Clemo d'ave
to stop the rats running up his trousers
in the bullock shed

*

#18 Flock of emus & old bird on Eggs

the giant birds squat on a nest
with their knocked knees you draw so well
and one with a snake sliding up behind un
a lot of birds by the river
and tracks of birds going up to heaven
bird heaven where they live the way they want
not shut underground or made to ride
at the station—is that a leaf?
a leaf in the air between
the blue birds and does one have
extra hair on his head, shaded light
and what's the nest made of
and do they all sit?

What didn't happen today

A chubby-legged poodle called Brandy didn't waddle across the oval

A gull didn't soar slow and alight

A woman didn't stand and gaze waiting for her dog to return

The sun didn't set over Black Mountain, fiery orange, burning yellow

A mynah bird didn't glide low across the path, or reach up to take seeds

A man didn't scrape a peppermint eucalypt leaf for menthol, or get
confused by a stick in the shape of a water dragon

He didn't savour the cool evening air and the single, long, whooping
bird call

Didn't grate extra cheese for semi-final night, or notice lemon balm
in the cracks between tiles in the courtyard, layers of grey in the ashen
night, ticking over like a faceless clock

Notes

The title poem was inspired by the documentary *Maidentrip* (CoPilot Pictures, 2013), directed by Jillian Schlesinge, about the single-handed round-the-world voyage of Laura Dekker, who was only fourteen years old when she set out and sixteen when she successfully completed her circumnavigation of the globe. In the film, we see footage which she shot herself of the parties she held to keep her spirits up. She would put on her favourite music and dance and cook something special. In one clip, she makes pancakes and throws the first one overboard as an offering to Neptune—I loved that gesture, and in some way these poems are all pancakes for Neptune, or offerings to some other god.

Notes on inspiration

'Welcome to the tables' and 'Erode' were inspired by Cori Beardsley's exhibition *Touch*, M16 Artspace, Canberra, 2015.

'Ayoub' responds to the patterns in works by Indigenous artists like Paddy Jaminji and Kitty Kantilla at the National Gallery of Australia (NGA). Trying to find a poetic parallel, I turned to Turkish rhythms for a solution. This poem begins in the 2/4 Ayoub rhythm DktkDT (DktkD) and, after four stanzas, switches to a syncopated version of this rhythm (DkkDktk) for two stanzas and then returns to the regular 2/4 beat.

'Skim (segmentivity, indeterminacy, components, messing with)' reacts to Ali Jane Smith's article, 'Poetry, Whatsoever: Blake, Blau DuPlessis, and an Expansive Definition of the Poem', published in *Cordite*. Although her ideas relate to performance, I used them to try to make a new kind of page poem.

The first section of 'Originary' replies to a desert scene from the Artists of the Great War Exhibition (2017), at the NGA. The second is inspired by an installation by Xu Zhen, Play 201301, a medieval castle suspended on ropes made entirely from bondage materials. The third was also from the Contemporary China exhibition (NGA, 2017).

'Riding' reacts to BBC News reports from the US about Trump's idea of building a wall around America and a rampaging killer in Kansas. The two stories are juxtaposed as you would experience different news items and further contrasted with more innocent events in Canberra—the link being that both locations involve helicopters.

Textual notes

'Returning, I check that things remain'
earts—Cornish dialect word for wild bilberries
'The Greensplat road'
burras—Cornish dialect for the mounds of sand that are one of the waste products of China clay mining
'Sitting'
koromiko—native New Zealand flowering plant in the hebe family
totara—native New Zealand podocarp
'A line of geese'
ponga—native New Zealand tree fern
koru—unfurling spiral pattern in native New Zealand tree fern

Acknowledgements

Thanks to the editors and publishers of the following venues in which these poems previously appeared:

21st AAWP Conference Proceedings, Anthropocene, Axon: Creative Explorations, Backstory, The Burrow, Fevers of the Mind, foam:e—it's poetry, Journal of Poetics Research, Kokako, Landfall, Meniscus, Other Terrain, Otoliths, Poetry New Zealand Yearbooks 2018-2021, Social Alternatives, TEXT: A Journal of Writing and Writing Courses and *Western Humanities Review*.

'What didn't happen today' was written for the anthology *No news: 90 poets reflect on a unique BBC newscast* (Recent Work Press, 2020).

'Toyscape' appeared in the anthology *Giant Steps* (Recent Work Press, 2019).

'Chasing the moon' was written for a video and poetry collaboration with Rosario Lopez, which screened at *The encyclopaedia of forgotten things,* University of Canberra Faculty of Arts & Design Staff Exhibition, Belconnen Arts Centre, 15 July-8 August, and at Poetry on the Move, University of Canberra, 12 September (both 2016).

O was written for the critical/creative paper 'Warp and weft: aesthetics of the poem as an artefact of experiences in time', set to music by Owen and sung as a round with Niloofar Fanaiyan, published in *TEXT*.

'Swipe' was published as a chapbook by Amersand Duck in 2015.

'Heat', 'Permablitz day' and 'Diagnosis' were written as part of a series of poems about public health issues for the *Croakey* blog.

'Letter to Oscar' was commissioned by the National Museum of Australia for their 'Collections and verse' exhibition, 2019.

Owen would like to thank Sue Peachey, Shane Strange, Phillip Hall, members of the Prose Poetry Project and the Canberra poetry community.

www.ingramcontent.com/pod-product-compliance
Ingram Content Group Australia Pty Ltd
76 Discovery Rd, Dandenong South VIC 3175, AU
AUHW020721050325
407891AU00005B/27